EARLY PEOPLES

THE MAYA

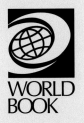

WORLD
BOOK

World Book
a Scott Fetzer company
Chicago
www.worldbookonline.com

World Book, Inc.
233 N. Michigan Avenue
Chicago, IL 60601
U.S.A.

For information about other World Book publications,
visit our Web site at http://www.worldbookonline.com or call
1-800-WORLDBK (967-5325).
For information about sales to schools and libraries,
call 1-800-975-3250 (United States), or 1-800-837-5365 (Canada).

Library of Congress Cataloging-in-Publication Data

The Maya.
   p. cm. -- (Early peoples)
   Includes index.
   Summary: "A discussion of the Maya, including who the people were,
   where they lived, the rise of civilization, social structure, religion, art and
   architecture, science and technology, daily life, and entertainment and
   sports. Features include timelines, fact boxes, glossary, list of recommended
   reading and web sites, and index"--Provided by publisher.
   ISBN 978-0-7166-2136-2
   1. Mayas--History--Juvenile literature. 2. Mayas--Social life and customs--
   Juvenile literature. I. World Book, Inc.
   F1435.M36 2009
   972.81'016--dc22

                                        2008039339

Printed in China
1 2 3 4 5 13 12 11 10 09

STAFF

EXECUTIVE COMMITTEE
President
  Paul A. Gazzolo
Vice President and Chief Marketing
Officer
  Patricia Ginnis
Vice President and Chief Financial Officer
  Donald D. Keller
Vice President and Editor in Chief
  Paul A. Kobasa
Director, Human Resources
  Bev Ecker
Chief Technology Officer
  Tim Hardy
Managing Director, International
  Benjamin Hinton

EDITORIAL
Editor in Chief
  Paul A. Kobasa
Associate Director, Supplementary
Publications
  Scott Thomas
Managing Editor, Supplementary
Publications
  Barbara A. Mayes
Senior Editor, Supplementary Publications
  Kristina Vaicikonis
Manager, Research, Supplementary
Publications
  Cheryl Graham

Manager, Contracts & Compliance
  (Rights & Permissions)
  Loranne K. Shields
Administrative Assistant
  Ethel Matthews
Editors
  Nicholas Kilzer
  Scott Richardson
  Christine Sullivan

GRAPHICS AND DESIGN
Associate Director
  Sandra M. Dyrlund
Manager,
  Tom Evans
Coordinator, Design Development and
Production
  Brenda B. Tropinski

EDITORIAL ADMINISTRATION
Director, Systems and Projects
  Tony Tills
Senior Manager, Publishing Operations
  Timothy Falk

PRODUCTION
Director, Manufacturing and Pre-Press
  Carma Fazio
Manufacturing Manager
  Steve Hueppchen
Production/Technology Manager
  Anne Fritzinger

Production Specialist
  Curley Hunter
Proofreader
  Emilie Schrage

MARKETING
Chief Marketing Officer
  Patricia Ginnis
Associate Director, School and Library
Marketing
  Jennifer Parello

Produced for World Book by
  White-Thomson Publishing Ltd.
  +44 (0)845 362 8240
  www.wtpub.co.uk
Steve White-Thomson, President

Writer: Lisa Klobuchar
Editor: Kelly Davis
Designer: Clare Nicholas
Photo Researcher: Amy Sparks
Map Artist: Stefan Chabluk
Illustrator: Adam Hook (p. 53)
Fact Checker: Charlene Rimsa
Proofreader: Catherine Gardner
Indexer: Nila Glikin

Consultant:
Arthur A. Demarest
Ingram Professor of Anthropology
Vanderbilt University, Tennessee

TABLE OF CONTENTS

Glossary There is a glossary on pages 60-61. Terms defined in the glossary are in type **that looks like this** on their first appearance on any spread (two facing pages).

Additional Resources Books for further reading and recommended Web sites are listed on page 62. Because of the nature of the Internet, some Web site addresses may have changed since publication. The publisher has no responsibility for any such changes or for the content of cited sources.

WHO WERE THE MAYA?

The Maya (*MAH yuh*) were an American Indian people who developed a magnificent **civilization** in **Mesoamerica,** a region of Mexico and Central America. Mesoamerica was home to a number of ancient **cultures,** and the Maya were one of several groups of American Indians there. The Olmec (*OHL mehk*), Toltec (*TOHL tehk*), and Aztec were some of the other important Indian groups of Mesoamerica.

The area in which the Maya lived was peopled for thousands of years before the beginning of the civilization that experts recognize as Mayan. Scholars date the beginning of Mayan civilization at around 1800 B.C., and they loosely divide Mayan history into periods, starting with the Preclassic. The Preclassic Period began around 1800 B.C. and ended around A.D. 250. The Classic Period, when scholars believe the Maya reached the peak of their culture, began around A.D. 250 and ended around A.D. 900. The Postclassic Period began around A.D. 900 and lasted to the early 1500's.

Before around 2000 B.C., the people who would become the Maya spoke a single language, which scholars call proto-Mayan. This single language

▼ The Temple of the Giant Jaguar, also known as Temple I, rises above the Great **Plaza** of the Mayan city of Tikal (*tee KAHL*), in Guatemala. The temple-topped pyramid is typical of building during the Classic Period of the Maya.

How Do We Know?

Archaeologists have studied many things made by the Maya, including the ruins of temples, palaces, and other buildings. **Artifacts** (*AHR tuh faktz*)—**murals** (*MYUR uhlz*), sculptures, pieces of pottery, carvings, tools, and such small objects as jewelry—are also of great interest to archaeologists. Scholars have learned a great deal about Mayan culture through their **codices** (*KOH duh seez*), as well. These folded books contained practical, scientific, religious, and historical information important to the Maya. Knowledge of Mayan culture in the Postclassic Period comes to us from written accounts. Some of these written accounts were made by the Maya, but others were written by Spanish missionaries and explorers. Spanish explorers had arrived in Mesoamerica in the 1500's.

▲ A stone carving illustrating one of the **rituals** the Mayan ruler Lord Bird Jaguar underwent when he came to the throne in the A.D. 700's. The king sits opposite his wife (left), who is performing a blood sacrifice by drawing a barbed rope through her tongue. Such carvings help archaeologists and historians piece together the story of the Mayan civilization.

splintered into the different languages that were spoken by the Maya, all of which belong to the Mayan language family. There are many languages in this family, including Itzá (*eet ZAH*), Mopán (*moh PAHN*), and Yucatec (*yoo keh tek*).

The Maya were an agricultural people who built cities of stone in the lowland **rain forests** of Mesoamerica. When first seen by European explorers, many of these cities had long been abandoned. The mystery of why the Maya left some of these beautiful cities is still being unraveled by scholars and **archaeologists** (*AHR kee OL uh jihstz*). The size of the buildings and structures in these Mayan cities was breathtaking—Mayan cities included ball courts, palaces, tombs, and massive temples built atop **pyramids**.

WHERE DID THE MAYA LIVE?

The Mayan homeland covered an area of about 120,000 square miles (310,000 square kilometers). Their territory was made up of the present-day Mexican states of Campeche *(kahm PAY chay)*, Yucatán *(yoo kuh TAHN)*, and Quintana Roo *(keen tahn uh ROH)* and parts of the states of Tabasco *(tuh BAS koh)* and Chiapas *(chee AHP uhs)*. Mayan lands also included areas that are now present-day Belize, much of Guatemala, and parts of El Salvador and Honduras.

There were three regions occupied by the Maya—the Guatemalan highlands, the lowlands, and the Yucatán. The heart of the Preclassic Mayan **civilization** centered on the lowlands in what is now northern Guatemala. Beginning in the A.D. 800's, toward the end of the Classic Period, the Maya began to leave their major centers in the lowlands. Eventually, they left most of this lowland region. Scholars are still trying to discover the reasons for this collapse of Classic Mayan society. After the collapse, some Maya moved north to live in cities in the lowlands of Yucatán. Others moved to the highlands of southern Guatemala.

The Lowlands

Lowland regions of **Mesoamerica** are located in a small section of present-day Mexico, as well as present-day Belize and northern Guatemala. This region lies less than 2,500 feet (760 meters) above sea level. Most of this lowland area would have been covered by lush **rain forest**. Limestone quarries *(KWAWR eez)* provided building materials.

▲ The ruins of the Mayan city of Tikal, in northeastern Guatemala, are overgrown with rain-forest vegetation. During the Classic Period, the lowland Maya built magnificent cities in this lush environment.

The Guatemalan Highlands

The Guatemalan highlands region stretched from present-day Chiapas in Mexico through what is now Guatemala and El Salvador. The mountainous highlands rise 10,000 feet (3,000 meters) above sea level in the central part of the Mayan region. The climate is mild all year round.

The Yucatán

The Yucatán region was located in the present-day Mexican states of Campeche, Yucatán, and Quintana Roo. Much of Yucatán was similar to the lowlands region in climate. However, the northern Yucatán was much drier than the lowland or highland regions.

AN UNSTEADY ENVIRONMENT

The Maya lived in a part of the world known for volcanoes and frequent earthquakes. Archaeological evidence reveals that large volcanic eruptions occurred in the highlands region during Mayan history. An eruption in about A.D. 200, near present-day San Salvador, El Salvador, destroyed everything within 18 to 30 miles (about 30 to 50 kilometers). An entire village was buried in about A.D. 650 near Ceren (*keh REHN*), El Salvador. Although tragic, these events have allowed **archaeologists** to learn a great deal about the Maya. The volcanic dust and ash preserved remains of everyday Mayan life. For example, the digging at Ceren uncovered preserved houses belonging to a farming community. At Ceren, a variety of **adobe** buildings used for different functions, such as living areas, storage areas, kitchens, and covered areas for making tools, were all built around an open courtyard.

◀ Mayan lands included all of present-day Belize and parts of modern-day El Salvador, Guatemala, Honduras, and Mexico.

The Origin of the Mayan Civilization

Archaeologists call the time immediately before the rise of the Mayan civilization the Archaic (*ahr KAY ihk*) Period. The Archaic lasted from about 8000 B.C. to about 1800 B.C.

▼ A Preclassic Mayan pot, made around 1000 B.C., was found in Colon *(koh LOHN)*, in present-day Honduras. The three-footed vessel with a spout is decorated with a human-looking face.

First Settlements

At the beginning of the Archaic, the ancestors of the Maya were hunter-gatherers—that is, they got all their food from the plants and animals that grew naturally in their environment. Eventually, the Mayan ancestors learned how to grow crops. Archaeologists have found traces of corn pollen in soil samples from this area, which indicate that people had begun to grow corn in regions of **Mesoamerica** well before 2000 B.C. By around 1800 B.C., the ancestors of the Maya had settled in the coastal and lowland areas of what is now the department (state) of El Petén (*ehl peh TEHN*) in Guatemala. These people came from surrounding areas—mostly from highlands to the west and south—in search of **fertile** land.

Civilization Arises

Many of the features of Mayan civilization slowly developed over the long Preclassic Period. Early Preclassic Mayan farmers lived in small villages, raising crops and gathering food from the surrounding forest. Later in the Preclassic period, the Maya developed more complex farming methods that allowed them to raise more food for a growing population. These methods included using fertilizer, crop rotation (changing one kind of crop for another on the same land), and building **terraced** fields. Increased crop production could support larger populations, and over time some Mayan villages grew into cities. By about 800 B.C., the Mayan lowlands were mostly settled. The Maya built their first large **pyramids** between 600 and 400 B.C. in some of these cities.

▲ Archaeologists at work on ruins in El Salvador. Much of what we know about the Maya, and about the civilizations before them, has come from archaeological finds.

Early City-States

By the late Preclassic Period, between 400 B.C. and A.D. 250, there were several large Mayan cities established in the lowlands, including Cobán (*koh BAHN*), Tikal, Palenque (*pah LAYN kay*), Calakmul (*kah lokh MOOL*), El Mirador (*ehl MEER uh dohr*), and Copán (*koh PAHN*).

TIMELINE

8000 B.C.–1800 B.C. Archaic Period

1800 B.C. First Mesoamerican civilizations begin to rise; Maya Preclassic civilization begins

1200 B.C.–400 B.C. Olmec civilization flourishes in Mexico

1800 B.C.–A.D. 250 Maya Preclassic Period

A.D. 250–900 Classic Period; Maya civilization at its height

A.D. 800–900 Classic Maya civilization collapses

A.D. 900–1200 Toltec empire rules central Mexico

A.D. 900–1500's Postclassic Period of the Maya

A.D. 1400's–1500's Aztec empire rules in southern and central Mexico

Early 1500's The Spanish invade Maya territory

1697 The Spanish conquer the last Mayan city

Mayan Civilization at Its Peak

Mayan **civilization** reached its height during the Classic Period, between about A.D. 250 and 900. According to **archaeologists,** this period shows the greatest development of Mayan **culture**.

The Culture of the Classic Period

The Maya founded their greatest cities during the Classic Period. Lively trade and effective farming methods gave the Maya a healthy **economy.** The Maya used a complex calendar, and they were skilled astronomers and mathematicians. They knew, for example, how to predict **eclipses** of the sun and moon.

In the Western **Hemisphere** (*HEHM uh sfihr*)— the half of the world that includes North and South America—the Maya were one of the first peoples to develop an advanced system of writing. Mayan writing took the form of **glyphs** (*glihfz*), or picture symbols. The Maya painted designs and glyphs on **murals,** on pottery, and in folded books called **codices.** They carved glyphs on stone monuments called **stelae** (*STEE lee*) to honor important events in the lives of their leaders.

Living in the Rain Forest

During the Classic Period, the Mayan civilization was centered in the tropical **rain forest** of the lowlands of what is now northern Guatemala. Many of the major Mayan cities, such as Piedras Negras (*pee AY drahs NAY grahs*), Tikal, and

◀ A wood carving celebrating the victory of Yik'in chan K'awiil (*yihk IHN CHAHN k ah WEEL*) over a rival king. The carving shows Yik'in chan K'awiil, who ruled Tikal in the A.D. 700's, in the center with glyphs on each side.

Uaxactún *(wah shahk TOON),* developed in this area. Throughout the Classic Period, populations grew and new cities were founded. Archaeologists estimate that by A.D. 750, the population of this region may have been 8 to 10 million people—much higher than it is today.

The Maya supported their large cities by using farming methods that enabled them to grow ample food in a rain-forest environment. Rain forests have thin soils and drenching rains that can make large-scale farming difficult. Despite this, the Maya were able to produce enough food for a huge population in a region thought to be unsuitable for farming. This is an achievement unique among both ancient and modern civilizations.

▼ The Avenue of the Dead and the **Pyramid** of the Sun at the site of Teotihuacan, a once-powerful city near present-day Mexico City. The people who lived at Teotihuacan had a strong influence on the culture of Tikal during the early Classic Period.

COMPETITION AMONG STATES

During the first 300 years of the Classic Period, the city of Teotihuacan *(tay oh tee wah KAHN),* near present-day Mexico City, had a strong influence on Mayan art, architecture, and weapons in the city of Tikal. Some of the people living at Teotihuacan may have been Mayan, in addition to the people living there from other **Mesoamerican** cultures, but Teotihuacan was not a Mayan city. Historians are not certain what the relationship between Tikal and Teotihuacan was. Some archaeologists believe that Teotihuacan conquered Tikal. Other archaeologists believe the cities were close trading partners.

SOCIAL CLASSES

As in almost all **cultures**, wealth, power, and prestige were not equally distributed in the Mayan **civilization**. A small group of **elites** *(ih LEETZ)* controlled most of the wealth and power. Most of the people were **commoners**. Mayan **social class** was determined by the class of a person's ancestors.

Wealth and Work

In the Classic Period, the separation between social classes was not as rigid. Mayan society had many levels of wealth. Evidence suggests that there may have been a middle class, made up of such workers as stonecutters, pottery painters, and **scribes**.

◄ A **terra-cotta** figure of an upper-class Mayan woman, made between A.D. 600 and 900. The statue shows the elaborate hairstyle and headdress worn by high-ranking women during the Classic Period. The raised areas seen on the lower face and the forehead were facial decorations created by scarring.

HOW DO WE KNOW?

Archaeologists have studied ruins and graves to learn about Mayan social classes. As is still true, the wealthy Mayans lived in homes that were larger than those of commoners. The houses of the rich were also made of sturdier materials, located in better areas, and contained more luxury goods.

Even in death, archaeologists can determine who was from the upper class and who was not. When ordinary people died, they were wrapped in straw mats with a few of their personal belongings and buried. Mayan rulers and other important people were buried in their finest clothing, usually in a tomb or in the base of a **pyramid**-temple. Servants were killed and buried with these elites, along with jewelry and utensils, for use in the next world.

There were a number of clear-cut differences between the upper and lower classes. The upper classes did not farm or perform hard labor (as the commoners did). Instead, upper-class Mayans managed the calendar and performed astronomy calculations. But members of the upper classes and lower classes could perform some of the same jobs. Scribes and **artisans**, for example, came from all levels of society.

Social Classes in the Postclassic Period

In the Postclassic Period, the separation between social classes became sharper. Each level had certain rights, roles, and responsibilities. Rulers, priests, warriors, merchants, and estate managers were part of the elite class. Some kings were more powerful than others, so there were levels even among the elite.

Most commoners were farmers, who worked and owned their own land. But, by Postclassic times, there were also landless peasants. These people worked land owned by members of the elite, and they were tied to the land. When the land was passed down from one elite generation to the next, the peasants were passed down with it. The people with the lowest status in the Postclassic Period were slaves. Slaves included commoners captured in war, criminals, and people who were sold into slavery to settle debts. Slaves were often sacrificed when their owners died.

▼ A painted vase, created during the Classic Period, depicts a servant (left) offering a vessel to a ruler.

THE ELITE

The ruler and other members of the **elite** class in Mayan society had many important responsibilities. They ran the government, waged war, studied astronomy, and maintained the calendar.

Elite Society

In Classic Mayan society, there were two elite classes: the ahaw *(ah HOW)* and the sahal *(sah HAHL)*. The ahaw, or lords, were the highest-ranking people in society. The highest of the ahaw were the kings and queens of **city-states**. The sahal were important under-lords who ruled smaller cities and assisted the ahaw in government, religious activities, and war.

Ancient texts report that many **scribes**, painters, and sculptors came from the highest ranks of elite society. They were the sons of kings and sometimes were kings themselves. Elite members also did other jobs that were open only to members of their class, such as city planning and trading.

▼ A stone carving from around A.D. 725 from the Mayan city of Yaxchilan *(yahsh chee LAHN)* depicts the ruler Itzamnaaj B'alam II *(eet sahm NAY b ah LAHM)* receiving a jaguar helmet from his wife K'ab'al Xoo *(k ahb AHL SHOO)*. Jaguars were a symbol of elite status in Mayan society.

SYMBOLS OF THE ELITE

Pelts of wild animals, especially the jaguar, were symbols of elite status and power. Jaguar pelts were used for everything from decorating thrones to the war costumes of elite warriors. An **archaeologist,** Kitty Emery of the Florida Museum of Natural History in Gainsville, has studied some 80,000 animal bones from more than 20 Mayan garbage heaps. Emery found that jaguars were plentiful from the period A.D. 600 to 900. But, as Classic Mayan **culture** fell into disorder, the number of available jaguars was greatly reduced. She believes that, as the situation became more unstable, elites needed more and more signs of their power and status, and the demand for jaguars became unsustainable.

Royal families lived in the Maya capitals in palaces (see pages 32–33). Other elite families had grand homes nearby. The houses of the elite were usually one-story, built on a low platform. When multiple-story houses were built, the upper stories were constructed like **terraces** upon the side of a hill or mound; a story was not built upon the ceiling of a story below. These buildings had many rooms that faced onto a courtyard. They were usually built of stone.

The Divine Lord

In the late A.D. 300's, rulers of some city-states began to take on the title of "divine lord," or k'uhul ahaw *(k ooh HOOL ah HOW)*. This tradition spread, and during the Classic Period, most city-states came to be ruled by a k'uhul ahaw. The k'uhul ahaw was more than just a king. He had to master many roles—including leader of the government, high priest, chief warrior, ball player, and star performer in **ritual** dances. By the time of the collapse of the Classic Period, this system of numerous k'uhul ahaws was no longer as dominant.

▲ ▶ **Terra-cotta** figures from the Classic Period depict a man and woman of the Mayan elite.

RELIGIOUS LEADERS

In Classic Period Mayan society, religious duties were carried out by rulers and **elites** who were recognized as **shamans**. The Classic Maya believed that all aspects of nature and life—including political events, social relationships, **economic** activities, and even a person's health and family relationships—were controlled by the gods. A shaman acted as a communicator between humans and the gods to gain favor from the gods, discover the meaning of events, and determine what the future would hold.

The Duties of Religious Authorities

Mayan religious practitioners worked closely with the rulers to meet the people's spiritual needs in many ways. Shamans communicated with the gods by various means, including casting marked beans (like dice) and using mind-altering plants and drinks to enter a trance state. Some shamans were religious authorities, more like priests, who had the important job of determining the luckiest days for ceremonies. Other shamans and priests gave advice, carried out **ritual** sacrifices, determined reasons for misfortunes, and foretold the future. High priests were called ah k'in *(ah k EEN)*, or "he of the sun." They conducted spectacular religious ceremonies and also acted as scholars, astronomers, mathematicians, and administrators.

Ceremonies often required the services of several priests. A priest called a chilam *(chee LAHM)* carried out human sacrifices with the help of four old men called chaks *(chawkz)* and another priest called a

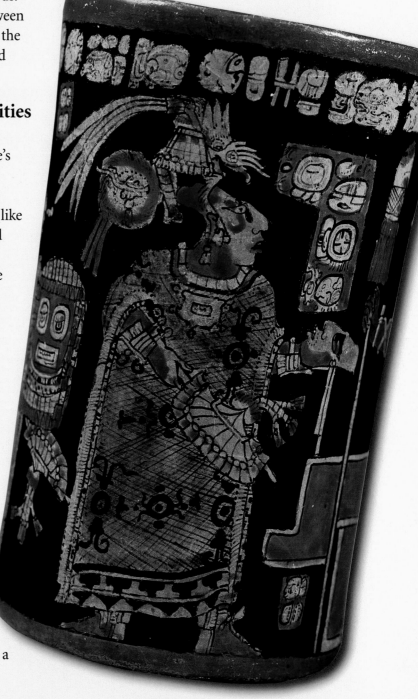

▼ A vase, found at Tikal, is decorated with the image of a priest. He is richly dressed in a patterned robe and an elaborate feathered headdress.

nacom *(nah KOHM)*. The chaks placed the victim on the altar and held his or her legs and arms. The nacom cut open the victim's chest and pulled out the heart. The chilam took the heart and spread the blood on a statue of the **deity** *(DEE uh tee)* being honored.

Becoming a Priest

Classic Period Mayan society did not have a distinct priestly class. By Postclassic Maya times, the priesthood was a full-time position open to those boys from the elite class who were not likely to become rulers. For example, younger sons of lords might become priests. In addition, Mayan priests were allowed to marry and have children, so many sons of priests followed their fathers into the priesthood. First, young boys would serve as **acolytes** *(AK uh lytz)*, helping a priest with his duties. Eventually, the acolyte might become a priest himself.

▶ A sculpture of a Mayan priest from the late Classic Period. He is shown wearing an extremely large headdress and ear plugs (large jewelry worn in the ears).

COMMONERS

In Mayan society, most **commoners** were farmers. Besides raising crops, farmers also carried on various kinds of trades and crafts part time. They made tools, pottery, and other useful items in their homes. In the cities, commoners worked as skilled **artisans** and traders.

Commoners and the Elite

Commoners had to give offerings of food and other produce to members of the **elite**. Food offerings included all kinds of farm produce, such as corn, fruits, and vegetables, and also fish, game, and cacao. Commoners also offered salt, cloth, **copal** *(KOH puhl)*, **jade**, honey, beeswax, and coral. In addition, they had to volunteer their labor each year to build public monuments and tend the lords' fields.

Homes of Commoners

Mayan farmers lived in rural homesteads or small villages near their fields. They built their houses from poles lashed together and used palm leaves or grass to thatch the roofs.

ANCESTORS AT HOME

The Maya worshiped their ancestors, so it was important to keep their remains close. When ordinary people died, they were buried beneath their own homes. At one house of Mayan commoners that was excavated by **archaeologists**, the burial had been performed in this fashion: A hole had been dug about 3 feet (1 meter) down into the dirt floor of the house. The deceased person had been buried and the grave closed. After a short time, archaeologists think the grave was reopened and the bones of the deceased were rearranged. Then, the grave was filled with a clay-based soil and covered with a slab of rock. This process prevented the grave from caving in as the deceased person decomposed, so there was no depression in the floor where people had been buried. The mouth of the dead person was filled with corn and with a jade bead that symbolized life.

▼ A reconstruction of the typical dwelling of a Mayan commoner. The walls are made of poles lashed together, and the roof is thatch.

◀ A fresco *(FREHS koh)*, or wall painting, shows a scene from the Yucatán in the Postclassic Period. The Gulf of Mexico was a source of food and provided a means of transportation for Mayan villagers who lived near the coast.

Houses of ordinary people were called na *(nah)*. Na were oblong or rectangular, and they were built on stone or mud platforms. These homes were rebuilt over and over again on the same sites and each one was occupied by the same family for generations.

A **nuclear family** lived in one house. Houses had areas for food preparation and craftworking, such as weaving and pottery making. **Extended families** lived in clusters of two to six dwellings called nalil *(nah LEEL)*. Some nalil were arranged around a central courtyard.

The Maya used the central courtyard or nearby platforms for work and other daily activities. Sometimes there were separate rooms or buildings that were used for cooking and such craft activities as pottery making, tool making, and weaving.

GOVERNMENT

The Maya were never united under a single central government. Each Mayan city governed its surrounding area, and some large cities controlled one or more smaller cities. But in the Postclassic Period, the governments of such cities as Chichén Itzá *(chee CHEHN eet SAH)* and Mayapán *(mah yah PAHN)* controlled large sections of the Mayan population.

Kings

Powerful kings first arose during the Preclassic Period. This tradition continued and spread during the Classic Period. Later kings often traced their family histories to the first ruler of a state, who was seen as the state's founder. In some cases, generations of a single family ruled for hundreds of years. For example, a series of at least 29 kings from one family ruled Tikal from before A.D. 300 to sometime after A.D. 869. A king would usually be succeeded by his younger brother or his son. Occasionally, a daughter of a king would become ruler.

Mayan kings had **economic,** social, and political ties with one another. They traded, went to war, and formed **alliances** through marriages and royal visits.

Advisory Councils

Mayan kings usually ruled with an advisory council. In the Postclassic Period, councils made up of heads of powerful families in the state ruled without a king. The head of each **elite** family held a particular office within the state government. These offices were passed down from generation to generation.

The head of a ceremonial center was called a halach uinic *(hah LACH wee NEEK)*, meaning "true man." He oversaw a system of officials that included judges, counselors, and governors of cities. When a ruler died, the elites decided as a group whether the ruler's heir, usually a brother or first-born son, had the right to take over the throne.

THE AH K'UHUN
One of the king's chief assistants was a high-ranking **scribe** called the ah k'uhun *(ah k oo HOON)*, or "he of the holy books." The statue (below) shows a scribe holding a pen and ink pot.

Local Government

Lesser elites were called batoles *(bah toh LAYS),* or "ax-bearers." They ruled smaller communities and were responsible for collecting payments from the **commoners** and keeping order. Various groups also operated at a local level to organize temple activities, trade, and police work.

▲ A palace complex encloses interior courtyards at Tikal. Mayan kings ruled their **city-states** from such complexes, which included royal residences as well as space for government departments.

WARFARE

By reading Mayan **inscriptions** and studying **murals** and **artifacts, archaeologists** have learned that warfare was an important part of Mayan society. Victory in war benefited Mayan **city-states** in a number of ways.

War for Reputation and Tribute

A Mayan ruler would often go to war to raise his reputation. A military victory was an important way for a city-state to prove its power and superiority over its rivals. The people looked up to their victorious rulers and felt secure in their power.

Competition for land, labor, and resources led different Mayan city-states to go to war against each other. The Maya also waged war to control **trade routes** or valuable mines. Receiving **tribute** from defeated states added to a ruler's reputation and wealth. In addition, victorious city-states forced captives to work for them, thus gaining a source of free labor.

▲ A Mayan mural illustrating a furiously fought battle among warriors armed with spears. The restored mural is from a series discovered in a palace at Bonampak *(boh nahm PAHK)*, in present-day Chiapas, Mexico. These murals record scenes from the life of the ruler Chan Muwan *(CHAHN moo WAHN)* from A.D. 790 to 792.

War for Religious Reasons

Finally, war also had religious meaning. The Maya believed that the gods determined who would win wars. Attacks and raids were often timed to take place on important anniversaries or at times when the planets and stars were in favorable positions.

The Maya believed that blood sacrifice was necessary to please the gods. Therefore, wars were waged to obtain captives for human sacrifice. Princes and kings went to battle to prove their worth by taking captives. Kings often added mention of their battle successes to their names. For example, the king Yaxun Balam IV *(yah SHOON bah LAHM)*, who lived in the 700's, added to his name the title Ah K'al Bak *(ah k ahl BAHK)*, meaning "He of the 20 Captives."

▶ A clay figure from the Classic Period depicts a warrior in a headdress representing a deer's head. **Elite** warriors went into battle in elaborate costumes that must have made them a terrifying sight to their enemies.

BELIEFS AND GODS

Religion was at the center of Mayan life. Everything in their world—from numbers to animals and landforms in the natural world—was filled with spiritual forces that were worthy of being worshiped. The Maya spent huge amounts of time and wealth building temples and tombs and carrying out ceremonies and **rituals**.

Basic World View

The Maya also believed that a sacred energy, or life force, ran through everything in the universe.

▼ A carving from Tikal of the rain god Chac, dating to around A.D. 600, is carved wood covered with colored plaster. The Maya often depicted Chac as a fanged, blunt-nosed crocodile.

This life force, called k'uh *(k OOH)*, was closely related to blood, so blood was sacred. Blood sacrifice was central to the Maya religion. The Maya believed that there was an understandable order to the universe and that events happened in predictable cycles. They timed their actions to fit with the movements of the sun, moon, stars, and planets. The Maya thought the universe was made up of three parts—Earth, the sky, and the underworld.

Ancestor worship was at the core of the Maya religion. The Maya believed that their ancestors helped them communicate with the gods.

MAIN MAYA GODS

Deity

Itzamná *(eet zahm NAH)*, a god with many functions

Chac *(chawk)*, the rain and storm god

Kinich Ahau *(kee NEECH ah HOW)*, the sun god

K'awil *(k ah WEEL)*, the god of kings and lightning

Yum Cimil *(yoom see MEEL)*, the corn god

Ah Puch *(ah POOCH)*, also called Kimi *(kee MEE)*, the death god

---

Ix Chel *(eesh CHEHL)*, rainbow goddess and moon goddess

Commoners worshiped their ancestors and offered sacrifices to them at household shrines. Rulers staged large-scale, public ceremonies to worship dead kings.

Deities

No **deity** (god) had a single form or appearance; most of them had many forms, both human and animal. For example, the Mayan god of death—Ah Puch—was sometimes pictured as a skeleton and other times as an owl. A deity could be male or female, could be connected to one of four directions, to a color, or to a force of nature, such as rain or thunder. It could rule over different areas of life. It could bring blessings or misfortune, depending on the calendar.

Pictured as	Ruled over
A toothless old man with an **obsidian** mirror	Writing, healing, priesthood
A fanged, blunt-nosed reptile, especially a crocodile	Creation of life, the number 13
A cross-eyed man with T-shaped front teeth and a curl at each corner of his mouth	The sun, kings, life, death and rebirth, the numbers 4 and 7
A man with an ax in his head, with a smoking tube coming out of his forehead, and a snake as one leg	Kings (K'awil is included as part of many kings' names) and lightning
A young man with a flattened, shaved head and often a corn headdress	Corn, life, prosperity, farming
A dead man covered with black circles, with bells in his hair and on his body	Death, war, human sacrifice, the number 10
An old woman with a snake headdress and jaguar claw hands; sometimes a young woman	Illness, death, fertility, childbirth, weaving, medicine

▲ The corn god, Yum Cimil, is depicted on a container for burning **copal** from Mayapán in the Postclassic Period. The Maya believed Yum Cimil brought good harvests and prosperity.

CEREMONIES AND FESTIVALS

Religion played a central part in the daily life of the Maya. The Maya believed that religious ceremonies pleased the gods and caused them to keep the Maya healthy, well fed, and safe from harm. Each day had special religious importance, and religious festivals in honor of particular gods took place throughout the year. The most important ceremonies and sacrifices marked the endings of the Maya time cycles, such as months, years, and longer periods made up of many years.

Private and Public Ceremonies

The Maya performed religious ceremonies privately in their homes and joined with the community for public ceremonies and festivals. At home, they offered objects to the gods and burned **copal** in their honor. They also offered their own blood, which they spattered on pieces of bark paper or wiped on statues of the gods. Spinning cotton and making corn dough for tortillas *(tawr TEE yuhz)* were also thought to be sacred activities.

Religious festivals provided one of the favorite forms of recreation for the Maya. These festivals were held on special days throughout the year, such as the Mayan New Year. Kings led these ceremonies. At these ceremonies, the king was expected to be both ruler and high priest, displaying magical powers and standing in for the gods.

Sacrificing to the Gods

The Maya regarded their gods as both helpful and harmful. To obtain the help of the gods, the Maya

▲ A stone figure, reclining, and likely holding a dish for offerings on its abdomen. These life-sized statues, known as chac mool *(chalk mool)*, are found in sites from the Postclassic Period.

CORONATIONS

When a new king was named, the Maya held a **coronation** ceremony to welcome him to the throne. The king was raised on a platform and given a royal headband, a rod that symbolized authority, known as a scepter *(SEHP tuhr)*, and other signs of kingship. He then took a new name that linked him with a **deity.**

fasted, prayed, and offered sacrifices. Ceremonies involving sacrifice occurred during all periods of Mayan history.

The Maya sometimes sacrificed animals to feed the gods. The Maya also practiced some human sacrifice, killing chosen individuals at such ceremonies as dedications of temples, to celebrate military victories, and at the funerals of great leaders. War captives were sacrificed after battles, and enemy kings and other nobles were especially prized as human sacrifices.

The Maya sacrificed people to the gods in numerous ways. At Chichén Itzá, people were sacrificed to the rain god by being thrown into a cenote *(seh NOH tay)*—a deep, round pool of water. War captives or ball players might have their heads cut off with a sword. For the New Year's ceremony, a victim might be taken to the top of a **pyramid** to have his or her heart cut out with a sacrificial knife. During the Classic Period, a captive was sometimes tied up tightly and used as a ball during the religious spectacle of a ball game (see pages 50–51).

▼ An artist's idea of the Mayan city of Tikal in about A.D. 750. A priest, in an elaborate headdress, is preparing for a ceremony.

CITIES

Rising from the dry lowlands of the Yucatán peninsula and hidden in the lush **rain forests** of Central America are the ruins of dozens of remarkable Mayan cities. Most of these ruins remain unexplored.

Many Mayan cities had tens of thousands of inhabitants. In addition, the populations swelled when people from the countryside gathered in cities for religious festivals and other important events. The two largest known cities of the Classic Period were Tikal and Calakmul. Other major Classic Period cities included Copán, in what is now southern Guatemala; Caracól *(kah rah KOHL)*, in present-day Belize; and Palenque, in Mexico.

Monumental Architecture

The ruins of many Mayan cities are spectacular, with large squares or **plazas** *(PLAH zuhz)* and huge stone **pyramids**, palaces, temples, tombs, and ball courts. **Archaeologists** call such large buildings **monumental architecture**. Monumental architecture of this nature could only have been designed and built by highly skilled architects.

▲ An aerial photograph shows the ruins of Chichén Itzá, a major Mayan city that covered about 2 square miles (5 square kilometers). The large pyramid in the center is called El Castillo *(ehl kah STEE yoh)*. The temple on top of El Castillo is reached by four staircases, one on each side of the pyramid.

City Layout

Often, the Maya built cities that were spread out over a large area. Buildings in these cities were separated by gardens, **reservoirs** *(REHZ uhr vwahrz)*, and orchards. The layout of Mayan cities was not orderly, because the Maya built outward from the center of a city over time. They arranged their buildings in groups around plazas.

The homes of the people surrounded the public areas. In some cities, such as Tikal, different plazas were linked by raised stone roads, or **causeways.** In others, such as Caracól, causeways linked the city with its "suburbs."

How They Built

The Maya developed special building methods to guard against flooding and the other problems caused by building cities on low or swampy ground. They built cities on areas of raised land and constructed their buildings—from the humblest homes to the grandest palaces— on platforms.

Most monumental buildings were made of limestone. However, some buildings were built from sandstone. Often, new, larger buildings were built on top of old ones. Monumental buildings were sometimes topped by roof combs—tall stone structures that added to the building's height.

▶ A model shows the layout of Tikal, with its huge central plaza. One of the largest Mayan cities, Tikal probably had a population of around 60,000 at its peak. Another 30,000 people lived in the area surrounding the city.

REPRESENTING THE WORLD

The Maya chose the locations and positions of their buildings to represent their idea of how the world was organized. Today, we organize maps by four cardinal *(KAHR duh nuhl)* directions—north, south, east, and west. The Mayan world recognized the four cardinal directions and added a fifth, which archaeologists named the axis mundi *(AK sihs MUHN dy)*. Axis mundi is a Latin term for "center of the world," and the Maya used a center in a building site to represent the sacred space of the world's center.

The Maya, for example, often built pyramids or other buildings on the east and west of a site to mark the path of the sun. A building on the south would stand for the underworld. A structure on the north represented the sky. All four of these structures would face into a central point on the site that was the axis mundi.

TEMPLES

The Maya built their first large **pyramids** between 600 and 400 B.C., during the middle of the Preclassic Period. Later in the Preclassic Period, between 400 B.C. and A.D. 250, several large Mayan settlements developed in the lowlands. Some of the largest Mayan pyramids were built in one of these settlements, at a site now called El Mirador, in northern Guatemala.

Temple Design

Like other Mayan buildings, the temples were constructed of limestone or sandstone. Some were built on platforms of mud or limestone rubble, with a room on top. The platform often had nine layers, which represented the nine layers of the Mayan underworld. A steep staircase, with narrow, high stairs, led to the top.

USES OF TEMPLES

Although temple-pyramids were huge, the interior of a temple was very small. They were not designed to hold many people, only a few priests. What took place inside a temple was secret. Maya royalty performed **rituals** in the temples, and these structures also served as royal burial places. The Temple of the Hieroglyphs, at Palenque, is the tomb of King Hanab Pakal (*ha NAHB pah KAHL*). He ruled from A.D. 615 to 683 and was buried in a sarcophagus (*sahr KOF uh guhs*), or stone coffin, deep inside the base of the pyramid.

▼ The Temple of the Sun, in present-day Chiapas, Mexico, honors the setting sun, warfare, and death. It is one of three similar temples built by the ruler K'inich Kan Balam II (*k ihn IHCH KAHN b ah LAHM*) in the late A.D. 600's.

The lowland and Yucatán Maya built tall temples on top of large pyramids. Such pyramids were meant to resemble mountains, and the small, cramped rooms in the temples were supposed to be like caves. The design imitated the natural mountains and caves where the highland Maya worshiped. The doorways of Mayan temples high above the ground represented the entrances to the places where the gods lived.

Some temples had **glyphs** carved into them. Often, stone temples, such as the temple at Cerros *(keh ROHS)* and the Rosalila *(roh sah LEE lah)* temple at Copán, were covered with **stucco** *(STUHK oh)* that was painted in green, red, white, and blue. Some temples had images of masks of gods made of stone or stucco. Usually, only traces of the stucco and the bright paint remain on the temples today.

▲ A decorative detail from a full-size reproduction of the temple known as Rosalila, at Copán, in present-day Honduras. An archaeologist who has extensively studied the temple named it Rosalila (Spanish for a rose-lilac shade) because of the color of its paint.

The Rosalila temple, in use in the late A.D. 500's, is something of an exception. Often, when a new Mayan ruler came to power, the temple built by the former ruler was torn down. The Rosalila temple was perhaps too sacred for such treatment. Instead, the Maya carefully buried Rosalila inside of another pyramid when they could no longer use it. When **archaeologist** Ricardo Agurcia Fasquelle *(ree KAHR doh ah goor SEE yuh fahs KWEHL ee)* excavated Rosalila in 1989, its paint and stucco were still in place. The temple's careful burial under mud, stone, and plaster preserved it and allowed its fragile paint to survive.

PALACES

The Maya built palaces where rulers and other nobles lived. Mayan palaces were large, low buildings. They were usually single storied and had several dozen rooms or more. One or more interior courtyards offered private outdoor space for rulers and members of their household. Palaces took up most of the space in Mayan city centers.

Rulers built their own sections of palaces on top of or beside old palaces, so the structures continued to grow, sometimes over hundreds of years. Like temples, palaces were built on platforms. Some palace buildings were made of stone. Others were made of pole and thatch, like the homes of most **commoners.**

▼ A palace, called the Nunnery Quadrangle, at Uxmal *(oosh MAHL)*, in present-day Yucatán, Mexico, is made up of four buildings around a large central courtyard. The north building (below) sits atop an 18-foot (5.5 meter) platform and is reached by a 90-foot (27.5-meter) wide staircase. The photograph was taken from atop the platform.

PALACE AT CANCUÉN

In February 2000, a team of **archaeologists** found the ruins of a huge palace in the ancient city of Cancuén *(kahn KWEHN)*, in present-day Guatemala. The palace, completed between A.D. 765 and 790, had three stories, more than 200 rooms, and 11 courtyards. The palace's walls were covered with **stucco** sculptures of kings and **deities**.

Earlier, in 1905 and again in the 1960's, scholars had found the site, but they did not recognize its true splendor because most of the palace lay hidden under a thick tangle of **rain-forest** trees, plants, and vines. Arthur Demarest, a professor at Vanderbilt University and the leader of the 2000 team, rediscovered the palace. In his explorations, he fell into it through a mass of vines and thick vegetation with a large nest of snakes in it. Not coincidentally, the name always given to the site by the modern Maya villagers was Cancuén, which means *nest of serpents* in the Q'eqchi' Maya language. "That's when I realized that the entire hill was a three-story building, and we were walking on top of the roof," he later told a reporter. Demarest returned with a team that began excavation work on the palace, the site surrounding it, and the area governed by the ruler who lived at the palace.

Uses of Palaces

Palaces served not only as the homes of rulers but also as the centers of government. Two palaces at Tikal were organized like a large government building might be, with space for many departments.

Palaces were busy places, which had comfortable rooms furnished with benches padded with large, jaguar-hide cushions. There, kings held **court**, surrounded by wives, lesser nobles, and jesters (clowns who amused rulers). They decided on legal matters and received **tribute**. Kings entertained official visitors at their palaces, staging entertainments with feasting and dancing. Such events helped kings form and preserve bonds with the rulers of other cities.

Palace Staff

Rulers had palace musicians, who played wood and conch-shell horns, drums, and other percussion instruments. There were dancers; attendants—people who waited upon the king—wearing large, stiff headdresses; **scribes;** and artists. Palaces also employed cooks, chocolate makers, housekeepers, and a variety of other support staff. A court dwarf sat in a place of honor near the throne.

▲ Federico Fahsen (left), a Guatemalan expert on Mayan **glyphs,** and Guatemalan archaeologist Paula Torres, are members of a team led by Arthur Demarest (see inset on page 32). The scientists clean a stone panel found at the ruins of Cancuén. The panel's beautiful carvings depict royal Mayan ceremonies. Fahsen has called the panel "one of the greatest masterpieces of Maya art ever discovered in Guatemala."

PAINTING AND SCULPTURE

The Maya were accomplished **artisans**, creating paintings, sculptures, and carvings of great beauty.

Painting

Most surviving Mayan painting is found on long-lasting articles, such as pottery and sometimes the walls of buildings. Mayan artists decorated walls with brightly colored **murals** that featured lifelike figures taking part in battles and festivals. Similar paintings appear on Mayan pottery.

Sculpture and Carving

The Maya were also master stone carvers. They had no metal tools, so they carved stone and ground stone with tools made of harder stones, such as

THE MURALS AT BONAMPAK

Most of the murals made by the Maya wore away long ago. But a few spectacular examples have survived. Murals in the palace at Bonampak, in present-day Chiapas, date to A.D. 791. Surprisingly, these murals were preserved by rain water. As rain water fell down the walls, over time the paintings were coated with a somewhat see-through layer of minerals. Local people showed the murals to a Western photographer in the 1940's. Soon after they were found, the images were carefully photographed, and replicas of the photos were painted. In the ensuing decades, some of the attempts to keep the murals safe have actually caused them more harm. A roof built over the paintings to protect them, for example, caused the minerals to harden on the wall, making the images more difficult to see. Modern infrared photography has allowed **archaeologists** to get a clearer idea of details of the Bonampak murals. The restored example below shows **court** musicians celebrating the naming of a royal heir.

granite and basalt. Carvings covered most surfaces on buildings and **stelae**. Such carvings glorified the state and the king. They told the histories of royal families and recorded **myths**.

The Maya also made small sculptures of clay and carved huge ones from stone. They modeled human figures of clay in the early Preclassic period. Many such statues have been found at a site called Jaina *(HY nuh)*, on an island off the Yucatán coast. Jaina sculptures show ordinary Maya grinding corn, weaving, and doing other tasks. By contrast, the large sculptures, some standing over 30 feet (about 9 meters) high, were carved with portraits of rulers.

In the late Preclassic Period and up to about A.D. 600 in the Classic Period, sculptors molded masks of gods and other figures from **stucco** to decorate the outsides of temples. Examples of stucco masks have been found at Cerros, Tikal, and other sites.

Jade

Mayan artisans made beautiful objects from a stone called **jade**. Most of the jade they used was green in color. Artisans cut jade by sawing it with sturdy cords covered with tiny pieces of harder stone. They drilled and carved jade with tools made of bone and wood.

▶ A jade **mosaic** *(moh ZAY ihk)* mask, found in the Temple of the **Inscriptions** at Palenque, was the burial mask of the ruler Pacal *(pah KAHL)*.

POTTERY

The Maya were among the world's most gifted potters. They are famous for the polished surfaces on their pottery. Mayan pottery was often colored in shades of red, orange, brown, and black. They also made wonderful painted vases during the Late Classic Period. They were the only **Mesoamericans** to use glazes, or glassy, baked-on finishes.

Archaeologists know little about how the Maya made their pottery. They have found no evidence of kilns (*kihlnz*), or ovens used to fire (heat) pottery. Most everyday pottery was made at home. However, some pottery was made by master **artisans**. In the Postclassic period, Mayan potters probably used molds to mass-produce pottery.

Pottery Styles

Mayan pottery styles changed over time. Typical Preclassic pottery was coated in red slip, a creamy mixture of clay, water, and coloring. Pottery coated in slip and fired has a slightly shiny surface. In the Classic Period, pottery was painted in different colors. The most common color combination was designs of red and black on a background of orange or cream. Such pottery was decorated with **glyphs**, geometric designs, and

◀ Mayan artisans of the Preclassical Period often designed vessels in the shapes of people. Ceramics from this period frequently have a waxy surface.

scenes of the gods or of kings with their **courts.** Postclassic pottery was covered in red or orange slip, and the surface was carved, etched, or modeled.

Pottery and the Elite

Giving gifts of painted vases was an important way for rulers to show their loyalty and friendship. They also entertained one another at ceremonial feasts. Archaeologists have identified special dishes in which food was served at such feasts.

▶ A vase painted with black glyphs and figures on a red background is identifiable as typical Mayan pottery made during the late Classic Period.

MATHEMATICS AND ASTRONOMY

Mathematics and astronomy were closely connected to religion for the Maya. They used their advanced knowledge of mathematics and astronomy to record the movements of the stars and planets and create a complex calendar. The calendar allowed the Maya to choose what they believed would be the proper days for everything from when to hold ceremonies to when to perform sacrifices, or when to plant crops.

Mathematical System

The Maya used a mathematical system based on the number 20, instead of 10 (as in the present-day decimal system). A dot represented the number one, a bar represented five, and special symbols represented zero. The Maya were among the first people to use a symbol for the idea of zero.

◀ The round building at Chichén Itzá, called El Caracól *(kahr uh KOHL),* is believed to have been used by Mayan astronomers as an observatory. Named for the spiral staircase inside the building, caracól is the Spanish word for "snail," an animal with a spiral shell. Openings in the walls of a small chamber at the top of El Caracól line up with important astronomical points.

Observing the Stars and Planets

Mayan astronomer-priests observed the positions of the sun, moon, stars, and planets. They watched them as they rose and set, and they recorded their positions. Their calculations and observations were made without instruments. They measured the positions of heavenly bodies by lining them up with buildings or hilltops. **Archaeologists** believe that the Maya set up simple sighting devices, such as crossed sticks, on high platforms.

Mayan astronomer-priests made tables predicting **eclipses** and the orbit of the planet Venus. They discovered that the stars and planets moved in cycles—that is, movements that repeated regularly. They used the cycles to create calendars. The Maya had calendars based on the sun and on the moon as well as calendars marking the cycles of Venus, Mars, and Jupiter. The Maya believed their knowledge of the movements of the stars and planets could be used to explain the past and to predict the future.

▶ A clay container for burning **copal** during **rituals.** The decoration, a symbol representing the first month of the Mayan calendar, indicates the close link between Mayan astronomy and religion.

OBSERVATORIES

Mayan architects built many buildings to align (line up) with astronomical events. For instance, many sites have a group of buildings that line up with the sunrise on the day on which a season begins. Windows in El Caracól line up with the rising and setting of Venus at certain times and the setting of the sun on days that have astronomical importance.

CALENDARS

Mayan religious authorities used mathematics and astronomy to develop several kinds of calendars. Calendars were extremely important to the Maya. They used them to determine when to hold the ceremonies that were at the center of their lives. One Mayan calendar was a sacred almanac *(AWL muh nak)*, or calendar of important events, of 260 days. Another was a 365-day calendar based on the solar year. For the Maya, the basic unit of time was the k'in *(k EEN)*, or day. The Maya also measured much longer spans of time by combining these two calendars. The 260-day calendar, the 365-day calendar, and the combined calendar were used by all **Mesoamerican** groups.

The Tzolk'in and the Haab

The 260-day sacred almanac was called the Tzolk'in *(tzohl KEEN)*. Each day in the Tzolk'in was named with 1 of 20 day names and was also given a number from 1 to 13. Each of the 20 day names had a god or goddess associated with it. The priests predicted good or bad luck by studying the

◄ A page from the *Madrid Codex*, a Mayan book created sometime between the 1100's and the 1400's. The Maya used this almanac to keep track of days in their 260-day **ritual** calendar. The **Codex's** paper was made from tree bark.

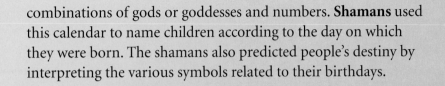

combinations of gods or goddesses and numbers. **Shamans** used this calendar to name children according to the day on which they were born. The shamans also predicted people's destiny by interpreting the various symbols related to their birthdays.

The Maya also had a calendar of 365 days called the Haab *(hahb)*. The Haab was based on the orbit of the Earth around the sun. According to this calendar, the year was divided into 18 months of 20 days each, plus 5 days at the end of the year, called the wayeb *(wah YAYB)*. The Maya considered the wayeb to be extremely unlucky. During that period, they fasted, made many sacrifices, and avoided unnecessary work.

The Calendar Round

Combining the Tzolk'in and the Haab gave a 52-year cycle called the Calendar Round. A Calendar Round date is made up of the Tzolk'in date plus the Haab date. The same combination of a specific Tzolk'in date with a specific Haab date only repeats once every 52 years.

◀ The outside walls of the Temple of the Masks, at Kabah *(kah BAH)*, in present-day Yucatán, Mexico, were carved during the Classic Period with 260 images of the rain god, Chac. There is one image of Chac for each day in the 260-day ritual calendar.

Writing

The Maya are the only ancient American people known to have fully developed a written language. They developed an advanced form of writing made up of many symbols—called **glyphs**.

Glyphs

The earliest examples of Mayan glyphs date from about A.D. 250. Mayan glyphs consisted of a combination of phonetic (sound) glyphs that stood for syllables and ideograms *(IHD ee uh gramz)*, or pictures, that stood for entire ideas or words.

▼ Glyphs carved on a stone **lintel** at Yaxchilan, Mexico, represent a particular date. The animals stand for blocks of time, and the profiles of gods stand for numbers. Together, the glyphs add up to the date A.D. Feb. 11, 526, in the modern calendar.

Carved and painted writing in Mayan glyphs has been preserved on pottery, jewelry, parts of buildings, and on large stone monuments called **stelae**.

Codices

Maya also wrote on paper made from fig bark. They recorded important information and sacred knowledge in folded books called **codices**. Even in Mayan times, codices and other writing on bark-paper did not survive long in the warm, wet climate.

Only three codices that are known to be authentic exist today in a state that allows them to be handled or read: the *Dresden Codex,* the *Paris Codex,* and the *Madrid Codex.* Scholars disagree on whether a fourth codex, called the *Grolier Codex,* is real or fake. The codices known to be genuine date from the 1100's to the early 1500's.

Later Writing

After the Spanish conquered the Maya in the 1500's, they would not allow Mayan **scribes** to use their traditional writing. The conquerors forced the Maya to use the alphabet used for Spanish, the Roman alphabet. Mayan scribes used the Roman alphabet to make versions of old documents. The most important Mayan work of this time was the *Popol Vuh,* written in the 1500's. The *Books of the Chilam Balam* ("Books of the Jaguar **Shaman**"), written later, include records of historical events and prophecies.

▲ Mayan glyphs from the *Madrid Codex.* The glyphs (running horizontally under the red line at the center of this image) are read from left to right. The bars and dots represent numbers.

FAMILY LIFE

Entire Mayan families, including parents, children, and grandparents, lived together as an **extended family**. Everyone in a household helped with the work. The men and the older boys in the family did most of the farm work, such as clearing and weeding the fields and planting the crops. They also did most of the hunting and fishing and made tools. The women and the older girls made the family's clothes, prepared meals, made pottery and baskets, raised the younger children, and supplied the house with firewood and water.

▼ A **terra-cotta** sculpture from the Classic Period depicts a woman weaving cloth on a loom.

ROLES OF WOMEN

Archaeologists and experts on the Maya have a difficult time understanding the roles that women played in Mayan **culture.** This is because women are seldom discussed in written Mayan records. Whether on **stelae,** in **codices,** or elsewhere, there is very little mention of women in any written source. In fact, archaeologists have found graves of **elite** Mayans in which there are two bodies buried—one male and one female, both accompanied by valuable goods—yet nowhere does the name of the woman appear at the tomb. Scholars assume the dead woman was the wife of the man buried there, but there is no way to verify this.

From what scholars do know, women cared for the house and the children and did the cooking. Women are also thought to have been the weavers of cloth. In some instances, scholars have found writings that describe women in positions of political or religious power.

Children

Children were highly valued and loved. Among ordinary people, girls helped their mother with household chores, weaving, and making pottery. Boys helped their father in the fields and on hunting and fishing trips. There is no evidence showing with what kinds of games or toys the Maya amused themselves.

In Postclassic times, ceremonies marked stages in children's lives. During a ceremony at age 4, a red shell was tied around a girl's waist and a white bead was attached to a boy's hair. Becoming an adult was marked by another ceremony, during which the bead and the shell were removed.

Young Women and Men

Women were expected to live with their parents until they married. Young unmarried men lived together in large houses. In the Postclassic Period, Maya were married at around the age of 20 to a spouse who had been chosen by their families when the bride and groom were children. Families often used the services of a professional matchmaker. A **shaman** performed the ceremony at the home of the bride's father. The groom lived in the home of his wife's parents. A lazy husband could be asked to move out. After several years, the couple would build a new house near the husband's family.

▲ A stele, carved in A.D. 730, honors the wife of a Mayan king. The sculpture is in Copán, in present-day Honduras.

CLOTHING AND PERSONAL APPEARANCE

Most Mayan art depicted, or showed, the **elite** classes, not **commoners**. Nevertheless, from what scholars can find out from Spanish sources, the descriptions here give a likely idea as to what Maya wore. The Maya in the hot, tropical lowlands mostly wore loincloths when working but wore more complete outfits at other times. The Maya wove garments from cotton or other fibers. Commoners and the elite wore similar articles of clothing. But in general, the clothing and accessories of the elite were richly decorated, while those of commoners may have just been embroidered with simple patterns.

Ordinary Dress

Men wore a loincloth, a strip of cloth tied with a belt or a sash around the hips and passed between the legs. They also wore a square of cloth around their shoulders called a pati *(pah TEE)*. Women wore a loose, ankle-length dress called a huipil *(wee PEEL)*. They decorated the hems and necklines of their huipil with colorful embroidery. In the Postclassic Period, women wore a piece of folded cloth tied around their chests, and a skirt below. The Maya wore sandals made of deer hide. The sandals were held on the feet by strips of hide between the first and second toes and the third and fourth toes. Commoners wore jewelry made of bone, wood, shell, or stone.

▲ ▶ Ear flares from the early Classic Period made of shell and decorated with the profile of a ruler. Commonly worn by the Mayan elite, ear flares were large disks that are thought to have been attached to a weighted cord that passed through the ear lobe.

Formal Fashion

For formal events, the common Maya wore more complete cotton clothing. The upper classes wore much finer clothes. They had splendid headdresses made from the brightly colored feathers of tropical birds. The long, shimmering feathers of the quetzal *(keht SAHL)* bird were used to make royal headdresses. The king's shoulder cloth, or pati, had feathers and jaguar pelts.

CROSSED EYES AND FLAT HEADS

The Maya had different ideas about beauty than the ideas that are common today. For example, they considered crossed eyes to be a sign of beauty. To achieve this effect, a mother in the Postclassic Period attached a small ball to a lock of her baby's hair, hanging between the eyes. Often, a child's eyes became permanently crossed from staring at the ball.

The Maya also flattened their babies' heads. By tying an infant's head between two boards during the time period when the skull bones were developing, the skull bones set and the flattening was permanent. The sloping forehead and pointed crown of the head can be seen in many people depicted in Mayan artwork. The statue of a woman on page 44 shows the result of such head shaping.

The elite also wore jewelry made of green **jade** and other stones, colorful shells, feathers, and the teeth and claws of jaguars.

Grooming and Adornments for the Elite

Men and women both wore their hair long. Both sexes wore turban-style head coverings, and often the hair was interwoven with the headdress. Men left a long piece of hair hanging down their back.

Body adornment was common. Unmarried men painted their bodies black. Married men and women tattooed themselves by painting the body with a design and then cutting the skin over that design. The paint entered the cut, and the paint and eventual scar formed the tattoo. People also beautified their teeth by filing them, etching them, and putting pieces of jade in them.

▲ A vase from Tikal depicts a member of the Mayan elite in ceremonial dress. He wears an ornate headdress sporting brightly colored feathers.

FOOD AND DRINK

The Maya had a healthy, varied diet. They farmed and raised animals, hunted and fished, and gathered wild foods. The tropical forests abounded in such wild game as deer, rabbits, birds, monkeys, a piglike animal known as a tapir *(TAY puhr)*, a kind of large rodent called an agouti *(uh GOO tee)*, and armadillos *(ahr muh DIHL ohz)*. The Maya hunted with bows and arrows, spears, blowguns, traps, and snares. Inland lakes and streams and coastal waters provided fish and shellfish.

Farming

The Maya were able to grow food in places that people cannot farm today without doing much environmental damage. Mayan farming methods were, however, much less destructive to the land. They dug ditches and canals in swampy lowlands to drain the soil. They then used the soil from the diggings to build raised fields in swamps and shallow lakes in which they grew crops. They dug muck from underwater to fertilize the fields. They built **reservoirs** for irrigation. On sloping land, farmers built **terraces** to hold the soil in place and walls to control water flow.

In some areas, Mayan farmers used a farming technique called swiddening *(SWIHD uh nihng)* to turn forest land into farm fields. At the end of the dry season, Mayan farmers cut down the smaller trees and burned

▲ In present-day Belize, corn, the staple of the Mayan diet, is still grown in **rain-forest** soils in a tropical climate.

dry plants to create fields. After a few seasons, the soil was no longer **fertile,** and they moved on to clear a new plot of land. This method, however, is not as environmentally sound for large populations as is farming with raised fields.

Mayan farmers raised corn, beans, squash, avocados, chili peppers, and sweet potatoes. Traces of household gardens discovered buried in volcanic ash at Cerén, El Salvador, show that the Mayans living there also planted root crops, such as cassava *(kuh SAH vuh),* and breadfruit and cacao trees near their homes. The seeds of the cacao tree were an important crop. The Maya used cacao seeds to make a chocolate drink that was reserved for **elites**, high-ranking warriors, and long-distance traders.

Cooking

The Mayan diet was similar to the diet in Mexico today. Corn was the chief food, and the women prepared it in a variety of ways. They made flat corn pancakes, which today are called tortillas, as a kind of bread. They stuffed cornmeal batter with meat and steamed it in cornhusks to make tamales *(tuh MAH lees).* The Maya also used corn to make an alcoholic drink called balche *(bol CHAY),* which they sweetened with honey and spiced with bark.

> **BEEKEEPING**
> Honey was such an important food for the Maya that they became expert beekeepers, even raising stingless bees. Beekeepers built special huts that housed from 100 to 200 hives. The beekeepers encouraged the production of the best-tasting honey by planting particular kinds of flowers near the hives.

▶ A container for burning **copal,** a tree resin that the Maya used as incense. The earthenware vessel in the shape of a human figure covered with cacao beans reveals the importance of the cacao tree to the Maya.

BALL AND BOARD GAMES

For the Maya, there was no real division between things that were sacred and things that were of the everyday world. Everything had religious significance for the Maya, and so it is no surprise that they often believed their games to be religious in nature. The most sacred of their games was a ball game. Stone ball courts were a major feature of Mayan capital cities. The Maya probably also played a board game called patolli *(pah TOHL lee)*, which had a use in certain religious **rituals**.

The Ball Game

The rules for the Mayan ball games are not fully known. The Maya played many versions of the game, with different rules, and built many different kinds of ball courts. In general, the object of the ball game was to move a rubber ball, likely from one end of the court to the other, without using the hands. The rubber ball was heavy, and players wore padding to protect their bodies from blows. In one version of the game, kings played against one another, dressed in fine ceremonial garments.

▼ The ball court at Uxmal, with its stone ring, is typical of the Postclassic style of playing field.

▶ A pottery vessel decorated with the figure of a ballplayer from the Classic Period. The ballplayer wears black body paint and heavy padding for protection.

Earlier ball courts, in the Classic Period, had sloping sides. Later, the walls of the court were vertical with stone rings, or sometimes carved stone markers, high up on each side at center court. Also, the ball was smaller in later times. Players tried to put the ball through the ring or to hit the marker with the ball. Most ball courts lacked places for spectators, though some had steps that could have seated several thousand. The largest Maya ball court, at Chichén Itzá, is about the size of an American football field (120 yards [110 meters] in length).

Sometimes, players were sacrificed after a game. At one time, experts thought the captain or the entire team that lost was sacrificed. Now, some think it was the captain or team that won who were sacrificed. The ball game had sacred meaning, and the winners would have been seen as a worthy sacrifice for the gods.

Patolli

Archaeologists have found examples of the ancient board game called patolli at Mayan sites. Patolli was played on a board divided into squares. Players threw beans or corn kernels with markings (similar to dice) to move around the board. The first person to travel all the way around the board was the winner. The Maya played the game for fun, for gambling, and in religious rituals.

THE HERO TWINS

The most important Mayan **myth** tells of the Hero Twins. The story begins with twin brothers being called to play a ball game against the lords of the underworld. The brothers are defeated and sacrificed. The head of one of the twins is cut off and hung in a tree. As a princess of the underworld walks by, the head spits into her hand. The princess becomes pregnant and is banished from the underworld. She then gives birth to the Hero Twins, who return to the underworld to fight the lords. They bring their father back to life. As the corn god, their father gives food to the world. The Hero Twins rise up to heaven; one is changed into the sun and the other into the planet Venus.

TRADE AND TRANSPORTATION

▲ An ancient jade ornament from a Mayan site in present-day Guatemala shows a ruler wearing a headdress in the shape of a monster. Precious items, such as jade, were often traded by the Maya during the Classic and Postclassic periods.

Trade connected the Mayan **city-states.** The Maya traded with American Indians in what is now central Mexico and with peoples to the southeast in Central America. The Maya traded over a number of different routes. Some of these **trade routes** went across land; others followed rivers and coastlines.

Early on, the Maya bartered, or exchanged, one kind of good for another. Communities specialized in making a particular type of good for trade, such as pottery or textiles. Regions also specialized in trading in products that were readily available, such as wood and salt. The Maya did not import much food, as most Mayan towns and cities produced all the food their people needed. Honey and cacao beans were food items, however, that were traded.

Trade Goods and Cultural Exchange

During the Classic Period, trade in luxury goods was widespread. Rulers and other members of the **elite** class traded feathers, **jade** and other precious stones, mirrors made from shiny minerals, such luxury foods as cacao beans, and objects made of **obsidian.** Such goods were signs of their wealth and power and were used for ceremonies. The lowland Maya exported handicrafts, forest and sea products, and jaguar pelts. They imported jade, obsidian, and quetzal feathers from other Maya who lived in the highlands of present-day Guatemala.

During the Postclassic period, trade and cultural exchange increased throughout the Maya region. Professional merchants carried on long-distance trade.

By this period, the Maya used a number of items—including cacao beans, jade beads, copper bells, and certain shells—as money for buying and selling.

Transportation

Maya carried most goods on their backs or in dug-out canoes on rivers. The canoes were huge and powered by many men with paddles. Although the Maya knew about the wheel, and made toys with wheels on them, they did not use wheeled carts for transporting people or goods.

▼ An artist's depiction of a Classic Period market in the city of Tikal. Although little evidence has yet been found proving the existence of markets, scholars believe that the Maya may have exchanged goods in busy marketplaces in their **plazas**, as many peoples of **Mesoamerica** do today.

THE TOLTEC

The Toltec established an empire in the highlands of central Mexico during the A.D. 900's. They were the dominant people in the region until 1200. Some of the buildings and artwork at the prehistoric Maya city of Chichén Itzá resemble those at the Toltec city of Tula *(TOO lah)*. **Archaeologists** are not certain why the resemblance between Chichén Itzá and Tula exists. At one time, experts on the Maya thought that the Toltec had conquered Chichén Itzá. Now, however, they think that many of the styles of buildings and **artifacts** in Chichén Itzá that seemed to have been influenced by the Toltec actually occurred at Chichén Itzá before they occurred at Tula. For now, most scholars think that the cities of Chichén Itzá and Tula traded with one another and their **cultures** influenced each other.

THE MYSTERY OF THE CLASSIC PERIOD COLLAPSE

Beginning in the A.D. 800's, the Maya began to abandon their major centers in the present-day lowlands of Guatemala. Cities in the southern part of the Mayan region were abandoned, while cities in the north rose to greater power. **Inscriptions** give no clues to the reasons for the collapse of the Classic Mayan **civilization**. Scholars have different theories as to why the collapse occurred.

Scarce Resources

Some scholars believe that a series of very serious **droughts** *(drowtz)* led to the collapse of Classic Mayan **culture** in the lowlands. There is evidence in the archaeological record showing that serious droughts did occur at this time. Thus, these scholars believe that it was unfavorable climate conditions that led the Maya to leave their cities in the lowlands.

Other experts disagree, and they think there was no one cause, but that a number of problems all came together and led to the collapse of Classic culture. Under this theory, drought is considered to be just one of the events that caused the collapse.

Scholars who follow the multiple-cause theory point to a number of factors. In the Classic Period, there were very large populations living in the **city-states**. Their agricultural systems had permitted the Maya to farm for hundreds of years without harming the **rain forest.** But, when serious droughts occurred, scholars think the Maya could not sustain this system. As the droughts began to affect agriculture, the Maya began to intensify the farming methods they used. The farming practices that had worked at a less intensive level, however, could not be used more

▼ A **stele** carved with an image of Smoke Shell, the 15th ruler of Copán, created in A.D. 761. Soon after this time, the Maya stopped creating stelae dedicated to kings in the great cities of the Classic Period.

▲ Ruins of the ancient city of Tikal. Like other cities of the Mayan Classic Period, Tikal began to decline in the A.D. 800's.

intensively without degrading the environment. The Maya were not able to grow enough food to feed their populations without harming the land.

The Collapse

Damaging wars began among the Mayan city-states, and the effects of these wars began to show in about 750. Populations began to shrink, as death rates rose and birth rates went down.

The Classic Mayan culture of the lowlands came to a close. After 830, no new major buildings were constructed. Few religious ceremonies—once vital to Mayan culture—were held. The last known carving from the heart of the Classic Mayan civilization was dated Jan. 15, 910. The people abandoned their once-magnificent cities.

FIGHTING AMONG CITY-STATES

Archaeologists have found evidence that fighting among the city-states became more common at the end of the Classic Period. For the previous 600 years, Mayan city-states had mostly been able to coexist peacefully. They fought against each other in small wars from time to time, after which the ruler of the conquered city-state was usually sacrificed. But for the most part, the city-states shared culture, traded, and did not destroy the other cities they defeated in war. At the end of the Classic Period, this situation changed, and the Maya became more warlike. Perhaps, according to some experts, scarce water and food forced the Mayan city-states to compete for resources.

THE POSTCLASSIC PERIOD AND AFTERWARD

Some scholars believe that many of the Mayan people from the abandoned cities settled in the Yucatán. Others migrated south to the highlands of what is now the Mexican state of Chiapas.

The Cities of the Yucatán

From about 750 to about 1050, the center of Mayan **civilization** was in the Yucatán, in Mexico. The most powerful cities there were Chichén Itzá, Uxmal, and Cobá *(koh BAH)*. Some scholars believe that the power of these cities grew in part as a result of immigration from the south. These cities had a lot in common with the Classic cities of the southern lowlands. Scholars consider them part of the end of the Classic Period.

Chichén Itzá declined by about 1050, and Mayapán *(my uh PAHN)* replaced it as the chief Mayan city. Although Mayapán never became as powerful as Chichén Itzá had been, it controlled much of Yucatán for another 200 years.

Postclassic Society

Along the Caribbean coast and in southern Guatemala's highlands, the Postclassic Maya civilization developed. The main cities in this region included Tulum *(TUH loom)*, in the Yucatán; Santa Rita, in present-day Belize; and Iximché *(eesh eem CHAY)*, in the highlands of present-day Guatemala. Postclassic Mayan cities were governed by a council of nobles, rather than a single,

▲ A **terra-cotta** container, for burning **copal**, in the form of the head of an old man. The vessel was created in Mayapán in the late Postclassic Period, when the Mayan civilization was nearing its end.

all-powerful king. The differences between the **social classes** became greater than they had been in the Classic Period. Cities were smaller but more densely populated. Farmers grew large amounts of a single crop and were able to sell what they did not need. As a result, long-distance, large-scale **trade routes** developed.

In about 1440, the leaders of some Mayan cities revolted against the Mayapán rulers and defeated them. Yucatán was then divided into separate warring states. About the same time, several Mayan states in the highlands of southern Guatemala used military force to dominate other Maya in that region.

The Spanish Conquest

In the early 1500's, Spanish conquerors invaded the Mayan territories. By the mid-1500's, they had overcome almost all the Maya. The Spanish used Mayan land and labor to enrich themselves. They forced the Maya to work on farms and in mines. The Maya suffered from diseases brought by Europeans and from exhaustion caused by hard labor. Some fled to isolated villages. The Spanish also tried to end traditional Mayan religion. Catholic missionaries converted the Maya to Roman Catholicism, sometimes by force.

PEDRO DE ALVARADO

The Spanish conquistador, or conqueror, Pedro de Alvarado invaded the Maya **city-states** of present-day Guatemala in 1523. He defeated them in 1524 and set up a Spanish government at what is now the city of Antigua. In 1525, after a fierce struggle, he conquered the Maya of El Salvador. He then helped found the Spanish capital, San Salvador. Alvarado served as governor of Guatemala until his death in 1541.

THE MAYA TODAY

▲ A Mayan **artisan** sells rugs and cloth at Chiapas, in present-day Mexico. Many living descendants of the Maya remain skilled in traditional crafts.

The Maya still live throughout their traditional homelands in Mexico and Central America. Some 20 Mayan groups live in the Yucatán and in present-day Belize and Guatemala. Most Maya, however, identify more strongly with their village than with a region or larger ethnic or language group.

Way of Life

Today, many people of this region speak one of some 25 to 30 languages that developed from the ancient Mayan language. Many descendants of the Maya farm in the same way as their ancestors, still growing corn, beans, and squash. These descendants follow a traditional lifestyle in many other ways, as well—wearing similar clothing, making traditional craft items, and following a mixture of both older Mayan religion and Roman Catholicism.

Reclaiming Mayan Heritage

Since the Spanish conquest in the 1500's, the Maya have had to struggle to retain their land. The Maya got some land back during the Mexican Revolution (1910–1920). More land was returned in the land reforms of the 1930's. In the 1990's, a Mayan political rights group called the Zapatista Army of National Liberation demanded improved living conditions for all of Mexico's Native peoples. They conducted an armed rebellion in Mexico's Chiapas state, but their movement had limited success.

Other Maya have worked to keep their **culture** alive. In the late 1990's, Mayan scholars helped start programs to teach speakers of Mayan languages the ancient Mayan writing system. Because the modern spoken Mayan language is similar to ancient Maya, the native speakers have been able to help the scholars understand ancient Mayan **inscriptions**.

MAYAN RELIGION

The religion practiced by many modern Mayan people is a mixture of the ancient Mayan religion and Roman Catholicism. Mayan people may have statues of Catholic saints in their homes and churches, but often the saints will have taken on the powers of old Mayan gods. For example, a statue of a Christian saint may be thought to be responsible for bringing rain and helping farmers, as the Mayan god Chac once did. **Shamans** are still at work in traditional Mayan villages. They are still responsible for healing people and keeping the Mayan calendar. Caves and mountains are still thought to be holy by the Mayan people, and prayers are offered up and incense burned at many small shrines that are still in use.

GLOSSARY

acolyte A youth who helps a priest to perform his work.

adobe Brick made of clay baked in the sun.

alliance A union formed by agreement, joining the interests of people or states.

archaeologist A scientist who studies the remains of past human **cultures.**

artifact An object or the remains of an object, such as a tool, made by people in the past.

artisan A person skilled in some industry or trade.

causeway A raised road or path, usually built across swampy, wet ground or shallow water.

city-state An independent state consisting of a city and the territories depending on it.

civilization The way of life in a society that features complex **economic,** governmental, and social systems.

codex An early book (plural, codices).

commoner An ordinary person in a society.

copal A hard resin—that is, a sticky, clear fluid—that flows from trees. Copal is made from tropical and subtropical trees and was burned as incense.

coronation The ceremony of crowning a king, queen, or emperor.

court The place where a king or emperor lives; also, the family, household, or followers of a king or emperor.

culture A society's arts, beliefs, customs, institutions, inventions, language, technology, and values.

deity A god.

drought A long period without rain.

eclipse The darkening of a heavenly body. An eclipse occurs when the shadow of one object in space falls on another object or when one object moves in front of another to block its light. A solar eclipse takes place when the sun appears to become dark as the moon passes between the sun and Earth. A lunar eclipse occurs when the moon darkens as it passes through Earth's shadow.

economy The entire system under which goods and services are made, distributed, and used in a **culture** or country.

economic Of or relating to the **economy.**

elite A member of the upper class of a society.

extended family A family that includes parents, children, grandparents, aunts, uncles, and cousins, all living together.

fertile Able to easily produce crops (when used about land or soil).

glyph A picture symbol in certain writing systems that could be used to stand for an idea, a sound, or a name.

hemisphere One half of a globe or sphere.

inscription Words or symbols written, carved, or engraved on a monument, sculpture, piece of pottery, or other object.

jade A hard, tough, and highly colored stone. Jade comes in a wide range of colors, including dark green, white, yellow, gray, red, and black.

lintel A horizontal beam or stone above a window or door.

Mesoamerica The area that covers what is today Mexico and Central America.

monumental architecture Large, important buildings such as palaces, temples, and tombs.

mosaic A design or picture that is made by pressing small pieces of colored glass or stone into a soft mortar.

mural A painting on the walls or ceilings of a building.

myth A sacred story.

nuclear family A family made up of parents and their unmarried sons and daughters.

obsidian A natural glass formed when hot lava flows onto the surface of Earth and cools quickly.

plaza A public square.

pyramid A large building or other structure with a square base and four smooth, triangular-shaped sides that come to a point at the top, or, in **Mesoamerica** and South America, that are flat at the top.

rain forest An area of tall trees growing in a region of year-round warmth and abundant rainfall. Almost all rain forests are located at or near the equator.

reservoir A place where water is collected and stored for use, especially an artificial basin created by damming a river.

ritual A solemn or important act or ceremony, often religious in nature.

scribe A specially trained person whose occupation is writing.

shaman A person believed to have powers that come from direct contact with spirits.

social class A group of people who share a common status or position in society. Social classes represent differences in wealth, power, employment, family background, and other qualities.

stele An upright slab or pillar of stone bearing an **inscription,** sculptured design, or the like (plural, stelae).

stucco A smooth plaster used for covering the walls of buildings and for shaping into building decorations.

terra cotta A type of baked clay used in many different ways. Terra cotta is often used in fine art—for example, vases, statues and statuettes, and decorations on buildings are sometimes made from terra cotta. It can also be used as a construction material.

terrace A small wall built by farmers to hold soil on a steep mountain slope.

terraced Built on a steep mountain slope and surrounded by a small wall (when used about a field).

trade route A system of roads and pathways along which goods are transported.

tribute Money or goods paid by one nation or group to another, in return for peace or protection.

ADDITIONAL RESOURCES

Books

Amazing Maya Inventions You Can Build Yourself
by Sheri Bell-Rehwoldt (Nomad Press, 2006)

The Ancient Maya
by Lila Perl (Franklin Watts, 2005)

The Ancient Maya: New Perspectives
by Heather McKillop (Norton, 2006)

Ancient Maya and Aztec Civilizations
by Marion Wood and Peter Mitchell (Chelsea House, 2007)

Daily Life in Maya Civilization
by Robert J. Sharer (Greenwood Press, 1996)

Web Sites

http://mayaruins.com/

http://www.historylink101.com/1/mayan/ancient_mayan.htm

http://www.kidskonnect.com/content/view/256/27/

http://www.kstrom.net/isk/maya/mayastor.html

http://www.popolvuh.ufm.edu/eng/Kakaw01.htm

http://www.webexhibits.org/calendars/calendar-mayan.html

INDEX

Acknowledgments

Alamy: 31 (J. Marshall/Tribaleye Images); **The Art Archive:** 8 (Honduras Institute Tegucigalpa/Alfredo Dagli Orti), 16 (Gianni Dagli Orti), 17 (National Anthropological Museum, Mexico/Gianni Dagli Orti), 19 (Yucatan Research Centre, Mexico/Mireille Vautier), 20 (Archaeological Museum, Copan, Honduras/Alfredo Dagli Orti), 21 (Gianni Dagli Orti), 22 (National Anthropological Museum, Mexico/Gianni Dagli Orti), 24 (Archaeological Museum, Tikal, Guatemala/Gianni Dagli Orti), 25 (Mireille Vautier), 29 (Archaeological and Ethnological Museum, Guatemala City/Gianni Dagli Orti), 32 (Gianni Dagli Orti), 36 (Honduras Institute Tegucigalpa/Alfredo Dagli Orti), 38 (Manuel Cohen), 39 (National Anthropological Museum, Mexico), 45 (Mireille Vautier), 47 (Gianni Dagli Orti), 56 (Mireille Vautier), 57 (Museo Colonial Antigua, Guatemala/Gianni Dagli Orti); **Bridgeman Art Library:** 41, 43, 49; **Corbis:** 4 (Jan Butchofsky-Houser), 6 (Keren Su), 9 (Luis Galdamez/Reuters), 11 (Angelo Hornak), 26 (Hans Georg Roth), 28 (Yann Arthus-Bertrand), 33 (Daniel LeClair/Reuters), 34 (Charles and Josette Lenars), 48 (Steve Kaufman), 50 (Macduff Everton), 54 (Upperhall Ltd./Robert Harding World Imagery), 55 (Jan Butchofsky-Houser), 58 (Philippe Giraud/Goodlook), 59 (Robert Mulder/Godong); **Shutterstock:** 30 (Marco Regalia); **Werner Forman Archive:** 1 (National Museum of Anthropology, Mexico City), 5 (British Museum, London), 10 (Museum fur Volkerkunde, Basel), 12 (Dr. Kurt Stavenhagen Collection, Mexico City), 13 (Edward H. Merrin Gallery, New York), 14 (National Museum of Anthropology, Mexico), 15 (Dallas Museum of Art), 18 (N.J. Saunders), 23 (Private Collection, New York), 35 (National Museum of Anthropology, Mexico City), 37 (Private Collection, New York), 40 (Museum of Americas, Madrid), 42 (National Museum of Anthropology, Mexico City), 44 (National Museum of Anthropology, Mexico City), 46 (David Bernstein, New York), 51 (Dallas Museum of Art), 52 (David Bernstein, New York); **World Book:** 27.

Cover image: **Alamy Images** (Charles Bowman)
Back cover image: **Shutterstock** (Joop Snijder, Jr.)